AF431102

Red... *a collection of love notes*

Copyright © 2019 by Richard Akita

All rights reserved. No part of this publication may be reproduced, distributed, or transmitted in any form or by any means, including photocopying, recording or other electronic or mechanical methods, without the prior written permission of the publisher, except in the case of brief quotations embodied in critical reviews and certain other non-commercial uses permitted by copyright law. For permission requests, write to the publisher, addressed "Attention: Permissions Coordinator," at the address below:

Richard Akita
P.O. BOX CT11163,
Cantonments
Accra, Ghana
Alternatively, visit www.richardakita.com

Ordering Information:
Quantity sales. Special discounts are available on quantity purchases by corporations, churches, schools, associations, and others. For details, contact the publisher at the address above, Email or call.
E-mail: info@richardakita.com
Call: 0263 588 160

Published by Launchpad Press

First Printing, February 2019

ISBN:978-9988-2-9252-2

Cover designed by Ryzard Akita

Edited by Alfred Selasi Dzah

Red

A Collection of Love Notes

Flexibility and agility all surrendered
to moments of memorable groans
Each encounter differently inspired
wrapped around to ensure hilted sensations,
released to melodious synchronised ecstasy

Dedicated to Najate Akita

Thank you for giving me the

joy to express my love to you

INTRODUCTION

Words are insidious, beautiful when influenced by emotion
and vital in expressing the very same emotions.

A habit cultivated from a desire to spark a smile has led me
express my appreciation and celebrate the finer things in my
life.

Can this be a sequel to my bestseller "Every day in Love?"

However, whilst you have Red in your hands why not explore
the colourful expressions of love, appreciation, and a mind that
verges on the borders of wild imagination.

Journey with me as I use vocabulary to describe my thoughts.

Enjoy the read.

CONTENTS

Dedication

Introduction

orning SPLASH

fternoon splendour

vening rush

Inducing Smiles

Moments of Reflection

PREPARATION for A Dip

RICHARD AKITA

Morning Splash

Inducing Smiles

Who Am I?

I am your constant companion.

I am your greatest helper or heaviest burden.

I will push you onward or drag you down to failure.

I am completely at your command.

Half the things you do you might just as well turn over to me,

and I will be able to do them quickly, correctly.

I am easily managed - you must merely be firm with me. Show

me exactly how you want something done, and after a few

lessons I will do it automatically.

I am the servant of all great people; and alas,
of all failures as well.

Those who are failures, I have made failures.

I am not a machine, though I work with all the precision of a

machine plus the intelligence of a human being.

You may run me for a profit or turn me for ruin

- it makes no difference to me.

Take me, train me, be firm with me,

and I will place the world at your feet.

Be easy with me and I will destroy you.

Who am I?

I AM HABIT - *Author unknown*

*Every morning the sun breaks through the night
with an orange glow.
Then announces the day by flooding its light.
None of these acts are difficult because that's its function.
When you see the bigness of your God
then all things become myopic.
Please be the awesomeness you are created to be.
You're blessed beyond your imagination and empowered to soar.*

Just because it's cloudy doesn't mean it will rain. Just because it's
tough doesn't mean you're unable to handle it.
Just because you're lonely doesn't mean you're alone.
The only just because is fixed on Jesus
for He alone is more than enough.
But because it's a beautiful morning just smile.
I just did

Change is painful yet not new,
changing your mind intensifies your focus,
changed hearts experiences an abundance
Don't resist change rather embrace it.
This may be your best gift to yourself.
Be good to yourself and be a change agent.

*Remember you're impacting
many silently and being celebrated openly.
Keep your focus and maximise every opportunity*

The crescendo of sounds that is higher than decibels.
The energy and passion, the moans and raising of hands.
The charged moments that's purely ecstatic,

the sheer joy of joined voice.
An all-night of sacrificial praise to the one and only God.
Well done for teaching me how to worship.

Greater is the gift of life but greatest is the gift of giving.
Give praise for His awesome present of life to you.
Let your praise cause a dance wave in His presence.
Have a fantastic Day

Clouds form and release water when it's heavy.
Beauty is formed and released in doses
to the admiring onlookers.
You ooze the bliss of gorgeousness
and captivate your audience.
Have a jaw dropping gorgeous day.

Locked in the keyless,
the heart locks the love
the eyes conceal the admiration
the lips whisper the affection.
Alternatives never match up
Comparisons never reaches the scales
Thumping thumps
Shaky shivering
Knocking knees
Butterfly belly
Jelly legs
Simple but amazingly gorgeous is the notion of love.
You're loved and adored. Have an awesome day

Moulded yet uncrafted.
the sculptor chiselled,
the stone screams in resistance
the hand bleeds whilst the brow sweats.
Imagery conjured from memory birthed
When descriptive lack your frame screams through
It whispers beauty
It exclaims swagger It oozes awesomeness
You are truly a masterpiece Fashioned to reflect
Have a fantastic day

Tick tock tick goes the clock.
Tick tock tick beats the heart.
May your Sunday be a slow gorgeousness
that causes you to soak in all its beauty.

*Never compelled to show
you my love and never asking
for anything in return.
Love you and have an amazing day.*

Courage doesn't roar
but sometimes the quiet voice that whispers
"TRY AGAIN "
Create your day today.
I just did mine

Gracious morning
We may have seen the shadow of victories
throughout this year but be assured
that a shadow is a reflection of substance.
Keep your focus on Him
who is the substance and sustainer of victory
and our eyes will acknowledge
the very victory we've craved for from now.
It's all about the NOW in Christ Jesus.
We have the victory

Afternoon Splendour

Moments of Reflection

Memories never fade,
Love keeps those memories we share alive.
Telling of the memories incites adoration.
To live is to impact
To impact is intrinsic to legacy.
Legacy is the memory of a life lived.
Aunty Elizabeth as we remember your departure,
we celebrate the opportunity of being part of you.
Thank you for the memories and legacy.
Love you and together we will rejoice in His presence

There's a simplicity that's etched in complexity
but softened by loving.
An amazing grace that empowers
but doesn't suffocate our will.
In the midst of unrelenting challenges,
we experience peace once we stay
our minds on Him.
He sings over us and installs joy freely,
so we can smile.
His strength is only perfected
in our weakness
Truly there's complexity.

Split, hidden within the crevices
is the secret protected.
Secret secretly yearn to be discovered.
A personality, a character intact.
The mind wanders but the heart stilled
by the beauty gazed with the eyes.
Splits faster than the clicks of the camera
Splits sweeter than opening
Splits discovered, yet undisclosed

Victorious living is not in "If only"
but an acceptance of the gift of victory.
You're victorious whatever your situation,
be encouraged because everything is subject to change.
Keep your focus and maximise every opportunity

It is only the human seed that evolves.
The cycle of life is rooted in the doings or impact
whether intentional or fate driven.
The acorn produces the oak tree, contributes to the
environment by way of filtering whilst becoming a
shelter for birds.
Humans produce their likeness, paradoxically the
contributions of the offspring are solely their
responsibility.

Controlling Control!!!
Snapped but unclicked,
the fluttering of eyelids
Momentarily time freezes
Captured purposefully.
Designed and shaped to reflect.
The welcome of the beaming cute smile
Unperturbed by the attention
because of the steely confidence
that's founded on originality.
Flawlessly unique
That's simply you

The crescendo of passion climaxes
to your journey.
Faster than the speed of light you are
conceived in darkness at hidden depth.
Dead to eternity
yet limboed in the developmental stages
of the warmth of a womb.
We die to the warmth of the womb to step into light.
Discovery is the aim and legacy the driving phenomenon
The finale is not our death to time
but our return to our original form.

Snuggled and in cosiness
but times and jealousy cause
the ticking away of moments.
Not only time but the sun is in a hurry
to show off your beauty.
Night struggles to hold on so you can
snooze just a minute more,
but your beauty is needed
to show off God's brilliance.
A yawn, a stretch, and a desire just to stay in bed
but your beauty is needed.
A moment of solitude that sets your day,
but your beauty is needed.
After the refreshing shower and dressing up
you're ready to unveil that which your admirers seek.

*Love is strange
It makes you feel oddly loved,
it makes you warm,
it makes you smile and sometimes cry,
it makes me miss my Son.
It makes your day sweet,
it makes you forgive,
it makes the world a better place.*
Well Ryzard,
I love you and that is sweet.

If it wasn't then, it was,
but if it is then it isn't.
The joys of words that tickle the brain
The inspiration that stirs
the fluency of rhymed words.
The girl, the lady, her beauty, her intelligence
is captured in the most adorable frame of gorgeousness.
She's mine and mine.
Exclusively not, but for now mine to nurture,
groom, and mentor.
Our moments, our memories, our creation.

Every day I look for ways to tell you
of your influence and impact.
Every thought focused on the life
and effects of your kindness.
Every memory looks deliberate yet unplanned.
Every eye becoming an admirer, me being chief admirer
Every action geared towards
the full manifestation of your brilliance
Thank you for the privilege
of allowing me into your space.

Just when nothing was good you;
Marcelle Mateki stepped in
and showed the world that
nothing is good until you add.
You are the absolute best
in adding value to nothing.
So, I celebrate you, for out of nothing
you have captured many admirers,
of which I am chief admirer.
Go girl you rock.

To say it beautifully you must whisper

\- Sotto Voce,

To appreciate its beauty, you must pay attention

\- Cuteness,

To enjoy you must spend time

\- Create,

To express love, you must be

\- YOU

Captured not by mechanical lenses
but stored in a memory far greater.
Adoration not fused by lust but love.
The flattering of pulses
breathtakingly edged by flawlessness.
The motions of motionless imagination.
Vivid yet subtle.
Creation bows to your awesomeness

Amidst the tragedy are learning opportunities.
The mind is fraught with a myriad of suggestions,
yet none more potent than doubt.
Accepting your flaws is just the beginning
to unveil your brilliance.
Encountered, influence only the cry of humanity

Your dependency is only tied to your interdependence

that frees you to independence.

Self-love is to admire your beauty

without flaunting it for attention

Self-love is the preservation of peace in turbulent times

Self-love is loving another equally and never beyond

Self-love is simply love

A smile never fades but ripples into history,
chalked on the tablet of our heart.
A memory never fades but embeds
the emotions to rekindle moments.
A girl, a lady, none other but my Swee,
keeps the smiles warm and a beauty to behold.
That's my sweetheart.

Countdowns are synchronised with time,

being you is not a countdown

because you add more to others.

The peace of God

that surpasses all understanding is your portion.

Time is never on a mission,

but you are and need to maximise the time you have.

Should I be jealous of

the sponge, soap, water, and towel?

Why should they get all the attention?

Why do they get to share our life even until death?

Why?

A truth was told about me.
My response was to deny it,
defend my stance, rebel, ridicule and misbelieve.

They continued to whisper the truth about me,
and I went around seeking affirmation
from humanity and trusted in collaboration.

Some broke my trust, others just hurt me,
whilst carelessly focusing on themselves they forgot that
someone had spoken the truth about me.

Once I believed, I knew regardless of humanities
inconsistencies I remain true to the truth about me.
I may fail but that's me learning.
I will keep trusting because that's me at my core best.
I will love for that truth has saved me from me.

Thank you, Jesus, for loving me before I became.

When the smile is lacking,

When the squeeze is harsh,

When beauty frowns,

Only because of nature's cycle.

When time lapse and relief is seen the smile comes

but the ever-present beauty remains.

A wise person never ignores
that which makes their life better.
If only luck was all we needed but
Mastering life requires
focus, action, and execution.

The clacking of the cockerel is not an alarm to wake up
but to confirm your hearing is alert.
Beauty is defined by you,
cleverness is demonstrated by you brilliantly.
Happiness is seen as you express it.

What do you think?

Nakedness was never the inspiration for it.

The images of selfies did not inspire it.

The mind played and

conjured only to get the heart to flatter.

It all started with a smile.

Moments become memories only when you create.

Wishes would stay aloof when action is void.

Motion and action do yield to demands.

What will your 31st December be remembered for?

The choice!

The decision!

The focus!

Happy New Year

Days will go by,
Months will gather the year,
Time will tick effortlessly
but activated within our world is
the emergence of your
brilliance and awesomeness.
As you celebrate the addition,
do same with your impact.

Be aware of your awesomeness

but never compromise on your impact.

Admirers are watching the unfolding of your brilliance

Onlookers are just in awe and me ....

Just checking on you

If only
If only the world was sweet
If only life gave in to our request
If only money grew on trees
If only I had more amazing friends
If only ageing was cancelled.
If only ....

Unseen yet sustaining
Unseen yet felt
Unseen yet insightful
Unseen yet creative
When the unseen is seen,
splendour will be
jaw dropping gorgeous

Splendid is the form and awesome is the girl
Pretty is her smile and sexiness is
embedded is her swagger.
Voices heard yet
voice soothing is her soft tones.

Never said, never missed
When you find someone, who is awesome
- just let them know.
Girl you're awesome
When you discover true beauty
don't just admire in a gaze,
- just say it.
Girl you're beautiful
When you miss someone,
DON'T type it

Discovery of oneself is paramount to self-love.
Never judge yourself through
the lenses of other opinions.
You're fearfully and
wonderfully gorgeous.

Your miracle is God's normality
Your doing is your normality
Your thanksgiving is your miracle of gratitude
Walk in your miracle today

Life really delivers.
It brought you into my life,
it allowed friendship to develop,
your life experiences only show
how strong you are.
Your tenacity is a testament to that.
Life truly delivers

A mellow

Within the flow of sweetness

there's a mellow sound.

The sound is reassuring to the point of comfort.

A mellow just to keep one wishing for more.

Fortune amassed yet incalculable.
Your beauty is simply sophisticated.
Your character carved out
of incidents and intentional.
Your impact is jaw dropping gorgeous.
Make today better.

Smarter than me, more creative than me.
An achiever and focused young man who reminds
me of me but much better than me.
My son, my protégé, my hero.
Love you Ryzard.

You're an excellent one
Irreplaceable in the midst of one
in your fears, your eyes speak elegance
and you remain an excellent Dad

Irreplaceable, foolishly unique,
cleverly brilliant,
irritatingly missed,
Profoundly awesome
Substituted by thyself

In pursuit you focus on the prize, not prizes
In working out you're fixed on
the singular objective of fitness
In eating it's not the size of the meal
but the depth of your stomach.
But in thinking it's your
beliefs that hinder or propel.
Quit trying and "DO"
Dreamed it, Living it

Desire change?
Awaken the desire
Stir the desires by acquiring knowledge
Feed desires appetite
Leverage desires cravings
Hit the bulls' eye through DOING.

All this love for me?
The music is bopping, the sound is crisp,
the mood ready,
the dancers nodding rhythmically,
the atmosphere charged,
my Swee smiling.

When hardness is not in thrust but servitude.
When masculinity has nothing to do
with muscles but character.
When a jawline attracts because of the
impeccable conjoining of words.
When the broadness of the hands
draws in a cuddle only to
hear the beating heart
Swee that's you

As we push the year into the history books
without any effort let's be mindful
of the very source of our creativity.
Embedded in us is the most potent power that
shapes our own space and
impacts our communities.
That power is in one ACT
DO
As the curtains draw on the year it opens up
tomorrow for your manifested vision.
Our mantra must speak loudest:
Dreamed it, LIVING it

A new day, a moment, an awareness,
and an opportunity.
Faded yet etched in the chronicles of
history is the yesterday we lived.
Seamlessly exhibited is a beauty
so flawless, a heart so loving.
The softness of kisses covering
every inch of smooth silky flesh.
The gorgeousness that makes
admirers do double take.
The girl, the lady, the woman all wrapped in the clothe
of sophistication whilst exhibiting simplicity.

There's a math I dislike,
Counting days away
Adding up undelivered hugs
Multiplying tickles
Dividing attention
Subtracting adventure from boredom
But ……………
Unscented are the memories aroused
yet infused by sweet perfume
and the contributions of loved ones
that causes smiles and laughter.
Now that makes math exciting

Evening Rush

Preparing for a Dip

When talking about pleasure fluids,

we can see it in the light

of Water Baptism

– A. S. Dzah

Hidden yet outlined is the shape that keep curiosity aroused.

The opportunity never arrives but the imagination

lingers on the thought of touching.

The naughty mind is quietened by the images,

whilst self-control is almost lost.

So, I'm not using the four-letter word today.

The voided void stirs the legal argument for recompense and

the memory jogger arouses the yearning to gaze without

staring at the frame of sheer cuteness.

When words express the tugging.

Twisted tongues, inquiring fingers,

Fingered yet no substitution for the inched head

A gentle stroller, A cool breeze of breath, arousing goose bumps,

Lip to nipple, tongue teasingly causing a piercing nerve brain

confusion, resulting in lubricative readiness.

Pinked within the darkest shades,

lipped for parting,

ridged to accentuate gyration to induce ejaculation

Bonelessly hard, profitably increased, wetly invitation

Trustingly smooth, Operational pleasure,

Discharged to normality

As words describes your beauty,

counting only sparks joyous moments of laughter,

partying and memory creation.

As you celebrate your birthday just remember

you are simply gorgeous and beautifully blessed.

When sweetness is not in sugar

but framed in an exquisite beauty.

When beauty is not the outward appearance,

but a deep-seated character embedded in love.

When sexiness needs a memory boost, I reference you.

When a kiss is smoother and wet is on another level.

When a cuddle revives

When a fragrance of sheer indulgence is

breathed off your body aroma.

You tingle my senses to the nth degree.

Swee you do it all.

So, a kiss I requested and a race you run.

Making references to moments

yet caught in that very moment.

An inch you gain vertically and the admirers' queue to gaze.

Enviable the look as I hug, nibble, and kiss your frame.

A snore so melodic,

A smile so encapsulating

A peace written by the soundness of sleep

Just knowing you're amazing keeps me smiling.

When love is not the question, yet the demanded

answer is love then don't sweat it because you're in love.

When beauty is not sought yet presents itself flawlessly

then don't resist it because you're gorgeous.

When I think of you and miss you

then I hug you in my heart for there, you're safe and stored

A preciousness, the meadows sparkling with beauty,

beaming with gorgeousness,

stunningly oozing a smile

that's worth more than a currency.

The joy of knowing is to behold

The coolest of nights.

Fingered chills, shivering embrace.

Duvet covers to warm.

The shifting and tossing but sleep is sweetest.

Fingered chills, shivering hugging

Body temperature increasingly good

In the absence of you.

Fingered chills, mind over matter.

Softly does it,

Soft to the touch yet tough to withstand

Soft to hear yet clarity to decipher,

Softly spoken yet words to stir,

Softly, softly the swagger impressed unintentionally,

Softly approach but don't mess,

Softly kissing yet venomous addiction,

Softly undiluted

Smoothly:

The silky touch was no comparison.

The glow of shades was no match

The smoothness of sounds was inaudible.

Yet in sheer brilliance you are simply beautiful

Amazed yet not surprised.

Never an expectation yet a desired outcome Unplanne

attraction yet oozing beauty.

Time took note and onlookers marked the moment.

Trapped in a thought but caged freely in a heart

Just thinking of you.

Thinking is critical

Thinking is everything but

the inspiration for thinking is

essentially the crux.

Can you be the reason for thinking

From the rooftop I will whisper your name and allow
the gentle breeze to carry my voice to you.
From the edge of sleep, I hang onto the
dream of holding you.
From memory I cherish our sweet moments together.
Just saying!!

Stepped in and disrupted time.

Your life thus far trajectories the greatness within.

From the peripheral we celebrate you.

The song of your beauty keeps me hooked.
The song from your amazing personality
keeps me desiring more.
The song from you is never in a rush
but simmers to the flute of love songs.

When sexiness is withheld

Many admirers cry

Others wish, but those who know

how to access relax.

Free your mind and sexiness of life becomes yours.

Cozied under the duvet with the expectation of a touch
The warm snuggles of the duvet
but the touch is far better.
Mindful fantasies are contagious
so just smile because I have the touch.
My touch reaches deeper than a hand because it
soothes the mind, warms the heart
and breaks into a smile.
The touch of sheer ecstasy.

Water is sneaky

It conditions you to trust fully

and then keeps you dependent.

Food is so addictive, but spices are the dealers

that whets the taste buds.

Beauty in its simplicity is heart-warming

and I love admiring you.

Love adds and multiplies in ways that the ordinary

mathematician can't equate.

My **Najate** has me in the right place.

Inspires me and stirs the absolute best

and adventurous me.

Missing you is unavoidable yet so empty.

A kiss is never enough

A hug is not long enough

Your presence is surely what makes the difference.

Enthralled by your beauty

Mesmerised by your gorgeousness

Captivated by your eyes

Smitten by your love.

Drawn into your intelligence.

Moments don't evaporate

by the whimsical wishes of others.

Moments are our reality of the outcomes of efforts.

Synchronised moments are truly more exciting

than the big bang theory.

Moments need creativity

Moments need planning

Thank you for the moments we've shared, cherished in

my heart, and sealed in my memory

I never knew I was stirring

the motive was simply clear

but marred with apprehension.
Would she accept my love or simply brush it away?

Love is never planned but lust is.
To graduate from infatuation to love without
compromise is what I have enjoyed.
Love is at its purest when we can love unreservedly
and that you do flawlessly.

Sleep is not a time to waste.

The silence, the snore, the snorting,

and cracklings of the pillows.

Sleep is the preparation for a fulfilled day

However, the joy that erupts knowing that a loved one i.

graced to see another day makes sleep wasteful.

The time we want to spend together and tease, dance

azonto backwards or upwards, the stories,

the memories ooohhh the memories.

Just that you know what you already know.

You I love

Simply be!
With alacrity, be extremely you,
with gumption ooze you,
tenaciously project you,
Sotto voce your beauty, simply be.
There's none and ever will be another like you.
Unique to the max.
I celebrate you.

The strangest thing when you miss a loved one
is the void you feel.
I woke up with you on my mind.
How I wish I could just hug you and look into those
beautiful eyes of yours and admire your amazing smile
then tune my ears to the unique sound of your laughter.

Just as gorgeousness is uniquely singular,
you my dear have all the hallmarks of glorious beauty in
character, mannerisms, kindness, and lots more.

I pray my sweetheart wakes up fully charged.

I pray for revitalisation and refreshments of body.

I pray for the moments that will cause her to smile.

I pray for those breath-taking awesome moments that

will get her to laugh heartily

I pray for total grace for today.

Love you Swee and have a great day.

What's the use of loving you when I can't show it?

What's the use of having my voice if I don't tell you I love you?

What's the use of words if I can't express, I love you?

What's the use of my eyes if I can't tell you how beautiful you are?

What's the use of my arms if I don't embrace you?

What's the use of advertising my love but never letting you know?

Tell me please, how do you love to be loved?

So, I can love you on point.

On standby

Your beautiful smile.

Your Elegance

Your Swagger

Your Kindness

Your awesome cuteness

Your laughter

What's my crime?

Loving you?

Admiring you?

Missing you?

I plead guilty to all the charges and

wish to be sentenced to a life close to you.

When I type I love you do you hear my voice whispering it to you?

When I say I miss you do you see the tears on my cheeks?

When I'm awestruck by your sheer beauty

do you hear my heart skip a beat?

How I wish you knew how much you mean to me.

Days, Time, Moments.

A yearning to see you but a distance to far,

A day is too long to wait but the distance to far,

A time in your presence but like the hands of the

clock a distance to far,

Hugging a pillow doesn't make up for your warm cuddles

Imaginary intimacy lacks the feel of another

A stare at a picture doesn't make up for a presence

A wink, a snore still needs a human to be closer

Thought of you and scribbled this;
Smooth, soft, tender, and gentle are the words
that describe your presence.
Cute, pretty, exquisite, eloquent, and beautiful
are the words that oozes in describing you

Moments slip into days that fade into weeks and amounts to

months but a distance to far

A wish, a hope but a distance to far

A smile to soothe, a picture to admire

but a person to feel all a distance to far

A combination of the two spells how mesmerised we your

admirers are in and out of your presence.

A joyful confusion erupts when you smile

and for that I'm just smitten

As the water touches your body, running all over you shudder a.

the thought and smile at the depth of your imagination.

You pour the soap into the sponge, lathering

only to scrub the sensual smoothness.

You rinse and step out to dry off the water then you smile again

but this time teasingly then you sigh

You're the epitome of brilliance and a true representation of

awesomeness that's why I'm hooked.

You're not a cake but Moorish

You're not food but fills

You're not water but satisfying

You're not a painting but adorable

You're not toffee but sweet

You're amazing and awesome

In between the smooth legs

is the treasure that parts into

a sweet melodious stimulator

where men sing off key

in response to an ecstatic pleasure.

Joyous for a moment

but lasting memories of a lifetime

You stepped in and disrupted time.

Your life thus far trajectories the greatness within.

Thank you for being awesome,

I celebrate you and so proud of you Swee.

You're remarkably gorgeous and amazingly breath taking.

My joy, my Swee, my girl.

Many make efforts with little success.

You make little effort yet achieve outstanding results.

When I look at your frame, I need no convincing that truly

you're the best description of beauty

Understated for great effects.

Simple yet stunningly attractive.

When inspiration is daft,
and words exude inadequacies,
the eyes tingle the nervous system
and jams the flow of sensibility.
Simply put, lust has taken hold of your reasoning.

A cry, a scream, the nodding of heads but ecstasy amiss

Mounds, gazelle, fawns,

mountains, valleys, and forest.

Interesting words to describe a body

The curvature of outlines that stirs up the mind

and heart to beat out of rhythm

simultaneously yet unsynchronised.

The imagination that sees before the eyes

inform the optical nerves.

The poetic injustices of uncoordinated words that causes a

second read for illumination.

Then the voice of reason evaporates until

self-control dominates.

That's just you - Swee

Can one be?

The simplicity of your essence.

The savour of your impact.

The brilliance of your contributions.

The splendour of servitude.

You remain the example I emulate.

Thank you for being the ONE

Just when you think you have,

then you notice there's one far exceedingly better.

Just when you think you've arrived you notice

there's one destination needing exploring.

But when you're linked to brilliance nothing else matches.

Waste not, Want not.

Love is never wasted when desired.

Love wants attention and affirmation.

Learning is always an addition.

Knowledge wants you addicted.

Waste not, want not,

just be ***YOU***

Beauty cried out.

Silently you carry out your duties.

In harmony you breeze through your task.

Flawlessly producing excellence.

An outward appearance of confidence.

A demeanour that exudes brilliance.

Whilst you never show off,

the beauty within you is expressed outwardly in a silent scream.

You are the epitome of beauty.

Yes, that's you.

Sleep never runs away

but because you are cute

it wants to share you

with the morning.

I heard the thundering sounds,

but the preceding lightening was missing.

I heard what sounded like an orchestra rehearsal of deep sound

but the rhythm was missing.

I heard the pillow cuddle your cute face

and the bed rejoice as you lay on it.

From the shores of Ghana to the very room

where we share our most intimate moments.

I could say it with words but today I want my actions to speak

not louder but softly in moans and arrrrrrhhhhhh.

Project 21 our target

A taste hooked,

A look glued,

A girl of indescribable beauty,

I am flawed by lack of vocabulary,

yet stirred thoughts,

full of admiration

If I got a penny for every time,

I think of you I will be a zillionaire.

If I got a penny for every time, I miss you,

I will be richer than my bank account balance.

Fortunately, it's a heart issue which cannot be quantified.

There's a math I dislike.

Counting days away

Adding up undelivered hugs

Multiplying tickles

Dividing attention

Subtracting adventure from boredom

Unscented are the memories,
aroused yet infused by sweet perfume.

Captured features

Unframed splendour

Untamed beauty

The smile exposure of a smile that causes

numerous neurological signals.

The beaming aroused cheeks sparkled

by the whiteness of teeth

Eyes that confirm unexpressed joy.

When working is not the motivation but pleasuring.

The body, shaped for exploring

My eyes were ahead of my hands, lips, and vocabulary.

Unclothed by my naughty eyes only to whet an appetite for the

reality of touch, feel and moans

The reason you remain in my heart.

If words could say it, are feelings needed?

If actions can perform it, are confirmation necessary?

Within the depth of a heart is the yearning of love,

Within the depth of the stomach food.

Feed the brain and the results are incomprehensibly amazing

Non-geographical yet treasured to heighten sensuality.

Peaked contours topped with an island

packed with nerve ends that tingle

Forested yet purposefully landscaped

to drive a blood rush for hardening boneless stiffness

Wet to receive, trustingly orgasmic

Flexibility and agility all surrendered

to moments of memorable groans

Each encounter differently inspired

Wrapped around to ensure hilted sensations

Released to melodious synchronised ecstasy

If you allow, it will slip
If you ignore, it will slip
If you do nothing, it will slip.
Normal is boring so keep your
scorecard, soar, secure, and above
all redefine the awesomeness
within you.
Keep the focus and soar pass the
daydreamers.
Have a great day